RIVER DREAM

RIVER DREAM

Poetry

AUDREY TANNER

Kinstu Books

River Dream
Copyright © 2025 by Audrey Tanner

Published by Kinstu Books in the USA

Revised Edition 2026

Cover design by Audrey Tanner using elements from Canva.com. Elements attributions: @ksuview via Canva.com; @sofiastd via Canva.com; @wikilmages from pixaby via Canva.com.

Ebook ISBN: 979-8-9896979-6-0
Paperback ISBN: 979-8-9896979-7-7
Hardcover ISBN: 979-8-9896979-8-4

To my brother Frankie 'The Kid' O'Rourke,
whose music makes my heart so very happy.

Contents

YELLOW, AS A ROSE

You might arrive
into a garden

or along a path
somewhere near a sea.

There, a rose bush knows
how you have become

weary with a karma-
laden soul. She saves

birthing a bud,
letting her rose-head

know just when
to welcome you.

All you need
is to arrive;

there is no story
for her knowing

how to open
from her roots

through soil
into day.

Just let her
whisper into you

an observation,
rose-yellow glow.

Take rose essence
into your heart

letting go
what is unnecessary,

a drive, a journey,
what you have carried.

Instead unpack
self-arriving

as you move into
her warmth,

her soft perception,
soul uncurling.

Here is how she
opens to you

as a yellow rosebud,
letting her shape

show how the form
of sun becomes

a soft curl of soul.
This is how

you can know her,
being as she is

in sunlight, shadows
of petals, rose gold.

Then you may arrive
into self, letting

a city, or a town,
or an occupation

flee from you.
Then, a yellow rose

becomes for you,
a softness amid thorns,

light, sun to sun,
all the substance

of quiescence woven
with the soul.

MORNING TREES

Here, you arrive
into trees; here,

the air is scented
with lavender

and eucalyptus, salt
from the sea. Here,

you reach arms
to sky as if

you could take
a primordial breath,

settle heartbeat into
leaves stirring, become.

You say
'It's been the trees

and the ocean
every single morning.'

Yes.
Always.

Eucalyptus and salt,
the lull of sea, sand,

a spill of cloud
across horizon;

this is all
that needs to be.

Maybe you take
a photograph;

maybe you try to etch
a feeling into self.

This is only to remember,
later, when you are home

and away from sea,
how the trees whispered

all the names of you,
calling you into their midst

to take root
into sacred ground.

RIVER SHADOWS

Here are your
karmas merging

with water,
alchemy begun,
gold afternoon,
shadows dissolving.
Here leaf dance

in water is gift,
Lakshmi's magic;
always she shows
you ways to drift
beyond shallows.

Here are your
karmas as leaf fall

flowing into sunlit
refractions, soft tumble
and watery grace.
On a bridge
in gold sunlight

shadows show
you as Lakshmi.
Gold-throned,
you transmute, lotus
patterns converging.

As leaf fall, in water,
you are more sunlight

than shadow, an amber
amulet of being
drifting in currents,
karmas tumbling
in shallow and deep.

You are at last
grace beyond grace,
Lakshmi, a temple,
koshas oscillating,
a slow river.

MOON CROSSING SKY

She moved, tracing
the arc of sky,

as a yellow rose
pressed into silver,

slivering sometimes
until her fullness

could be shown to you,
through clouds

hinting the shades
of floral lavenders,

as a pearl the color
of calla.

In the morning,
with the red sun

raising itself into
being, showing sunlight

under the white
of gulls' wings beating;

into this she moved
slower, slowing,

hanging onto the last
moments of night

so that you
could see her.

There was a moment
before she moved

crossing sky
over oceans

into another dream,
another time zone,

a different continent;
she waited as you woke;

she hung in the sky,
fading into the blue

for you to know
how she's still with you.

PARABLES, IF THEN?

Now

The difference
between past lifetimes

and now
is as simple as

an act of sitting
quietly beneath

brilliant sun
on a sandy stretch

of beach by
a swaying ocean.

Then

A choice
to be born

is as much
a soft invitation

as it is
a vast parable

to be written
among clouds,

oceans, and
weathered shores.

Clouds

See how clouds
gather karmas

into the shapes
of being?

How many times
in a lifetime

can karmas be wrung
so that tears

of rain come pouring
from the soul?

Sky

Into sky
gulls swing

into loops,
gliding

with wings
extended

like angels,
manifesting

wind into
currents of joy.

Sand

Everything
becomes like this:

rocks worn
down to pebble,

an essence of grit,
a granule of sand meeting

grain upon grain
until granules become

a hill of sand, a dune,
a whole beach.

Drift

Why search
for whole shells

when equal wonder
is also found

in tiny bits
of scallop and clam

as have been
carried as drift

onto shore
by waves?

Sift

Sifting through
sand, perhaps

a found piece
of colorful

stone or a bit
of seashell

can suffice
to hold an entire day

at the beach
in its fullness.

CALLAS GROWING

Not far from ocean
the song of streams

singing themselves
into air is some

sort of chant,
an invitation.

Into this, you are
always drawn

as bees are drawn
into the magic scent

of calla, sweet curl
of lily, and into

the essence you
have always been,

honey-souled,
unfurling.

You are not even
five kilometers

from the sea and yet
here callas grow,

open as waves
of green leaves

and white bud,
unfurl as if

sails lifting into
breeze, curl into

some form
of a magic dance

in the peaty dirt,
by a soft stream,

near a hillside,
near a sea.

Always there is
the song of water,

then, roots of green,
calla, leaves growing.

Everything begins
with melody:

a moment to see
how your hand shapes

itself into a curve
as if holding

the shape of holding.
Into this, you may

place a stream,
air that smells

of muddy roots,
a hint of sea.

Already you know
the song of water

moving over small rocks
and into eddies

pooling near a hillside.
So too, you know air,

how it comes
into you with hints

of moss, sedge, a soft
decay of last autumn's

lingering leaves.
Then, you can

know this: the color
of green leaves spiraling

into form, calla
beginning.

There has always been
you, calla, calla, you.

All of your life
has been knowing

the curl of leaf
and stalk; your body,

breath, the way
thoughts form and

release as voice into air
to sing names

of things so that
they become

inexorable melodies
of water and earth,

plant and flower,
body and heart.

TREES IN TIME

In a past life
you were, perhaps,

a flowering tree,
one whose bloom

filled the air
with sweet mystery.

You watered yourself
with tears

but salt formed
a ring around

the trunk of you;
the petals

of self faltered,
fell down like rain.

You wreathed
your head

in tiny blooms
of olives and spice,

but the trunk
of you grew thick

and ringed
while the roots of you

burrowed deep
into earth as if to say

bloom and leaves are
too delicate, mere

shadow songs
of self.

Once you were
autumnal maple

with leaves as
hues of sun,

as wildfire,
as burn of deep reds

and yellow until
you scorched self

from yourself
and fell

leaf upon leaf,
a tapestry

of cinder shadows
on forest's floor.

There was a time
you chose

to be evergreen,
soft and with the scent

of pine. The body
then was lush

and spilling down
a multitude

of slender leaves
and cones

of self. Into this,
you dripped your soul

until amber sap
became gemstone.

Moonrise shattered
your tree-heart,

so beautiful the light,
and rings,

hues of rose-gold
and silver-pink.

You shed your tree leaves
one by one,

forming a pile
of self on dry ground.

You waited for daylight,
and rain,

for decay, to bring
another birth.

A RIVER IS IN IT

(a poem after Hermann Hesse's
classic tale Siddhartha)

Somewhere
in the interior

of the country
of you

is a mountain
where snow

melts into
a river of you.

Until you can know
this, you just want

to sleep
as Siddhartha slept,

to dream a
cool river's wash

of bare feet,
of weary body,

wanting a river
to flow.

Gather a water
drop of snow melt

into yourself;
gather rivulets

and streams
until you are a river

and full enough
to pour down

a mountain of self
into dream.

Dream yourself
as you want to be,

confluent, alive,
a water form of you.

Then you can be in it;
a stream, a river

moving downstream
into eddies

and pools, into deep
currents of self.

You might wake
as Siddhartha woke,

opening onto
a soft river bank;

then you may see
how snow melt

and heart melt
gathers until

it becomes a river,
fullness of you.

BLUE, AS A MOON

The sky filled,
blue moon, a dream;

moon, a mysterious
magnet that spun
you into soft light.

Mirror self, you reached
into night, through space,
finding a way to pull
moon into you.

There in the night,
a river of stars;

in the blue night
your dress
was cotton cloud;

mirror soul, you reached
into night's river
to adorn jewels
of galaxies onto you.

Into night, your ascent,
moon blue,

star river;
gathering galaxies
into the pull of you;

dream, a dance
in soft light begun—
woman, universe,
one soul in the spin.

PARABLES, THEN WHY?

Tide

As the moon
rises into night,

there is as much
a tide of ocean
as a tide of heart
coming into
the shore of self.

Shape

When the moon
wanders sky, you too

wander. When you
hide you are like
clouds that hide
the shape of moon,
the self at midnight.

Night

You too are like
a moon

at midnight, crossing
vast reaches
of empty space
in order to
find your heart.

Daydream

Your heart is
in the moon, too,

dreaming as
the moon dreams.
It is a dream of
homecoming,
waking into day.

Dream

You need only sleep
beneath a full moon

to dream, to know
how the heart
becomes as soft
as moonlight
and night flowers.

Heartbeat

As months
come and go

in lunar cycle,
within the moon
are dreams
of your heartbeats
that fill each moment.

Soft

The moon and you
may become

kindred mirrors
of the self; every
heartbeat a becoming,
each a dream
of shadow and love.

LAVENDER, IN SUNLIGHT

This is how
it may begin:
the color of dusk-purple

as a thought, the idea
of flowers. Stalks
and roots become full,

a way to define a manner
of being, simple dharmas.

In a garden you may
hesitate, noticing
the stories

that stalks, leaves,
flower-heads spin.
These are only

thoughts upon thoughts,
simple dramas.

Sitting in sunlight,
you may meditate,
somehow awaiting

the merge of lavender
scent and sky, only
to become spun,

thought into thought,
dramas of self.

This is how
you become lost,
hoping you can become

other than thought,
dusky floral heads
instead of your drama,

lavender growing
into your dharma.

Today, you should
just slow the breath
and wait until

dusky flowers bloom.
Forget about roots,
dharma. Forget

that you are also
trying to reach sky.

Just sit and know
sunshine on lavender;
you can then gather

subtle thoughts
and wildflower drama,
simple dharmas

into dream pillows,
floral scent of being.

You do not need
to think about this
to know that dramas

and dharmas
are alike, scent
fused in air,

fragrance
of the same bloom.

FOREST TEMPLE

Step into woods
as if stepping
with reverence,
with care.

Here a temple
manifests itself,

grown from roots
spread in soil.
Walk into this
as if walking into
sacred self.

Step into woods,
into a church,
a cathedral
of self, wood hewn

centuries old
from trees of the self.

Here you can be
as slow and quiet
as a tree. Here, you can
kneel into a forest
of self.

Wander a bit
with the slow steps
of a tourist,
letting scenery
merge into self.

Touch bark as
smooth pews,

rough limbs as railings,
all carved altars.

Step into woods
to reclaim yourself,
to kneel
as a parishioner
of self.

Then sit.
Then take in how

the scent of forest
connotes incense
as you burn
ash from self,
smoke lifting.

Into a community
of forest
there are all connections
of root to limbs,
limbs to leaves,

leaves to air,
breath and body.

Here is a temple
of self,

untouched, unadorned,
as intricate treasure,
root twist and burl,
a slow canopy
of being.

RIVER DREAM

While you slept
the moon rose,
half a disc.

Hidden in
cloud's shadows
the moon still

kissed light
into the form
of dream. Into your
shuttered eyes

her touch was
a silver river,
a melody of water.

Her kiss, the moon,
you dreamed,
falling through clouds
into slow swirl, a river

with silver banks.
You floated past
callas rooted

into muddy shoals,
whose white lips
in the moonlight

and night breeze
were a poem whispered
into blue-dark night.

Into the blue-dark air
you whispered,
chanting mantra as if

the voice were scents
of callas and water,
music of the breeze,

while the moon's
subtle shadows of self
were a river slowing

into whorls and drift,
into the soft touch
of a dream becoming
a dream of waking.

PARABLES, WHEN HERE?

Strands

Define, now,
that you are here,
how rajas in the park

is the sound
of dogs barking,
water flowing.

Roots

A park bench
invites sitting,
but you define,

now, tamas in
the inert sense
of dirt into which

only love,
truth beyond truth,
can be planted.

Sun

Shed an idea
of ideas. Then
sattva is there

always,
now,
in the way

sunshine warms,
inherent sky, source,
a sense of earth

and sun dance,
the layering of being
into seasons.

Proof

Touch a tree,
the texture of
body, hand,

soft stretch of skin
above sweet
bones meeting

tree substance, bark
softly flaking
away pieces

of self. Here, unpeeling,
a connection, a chance
to know everything.

Here Now

Then, here, now:
do not define it.
Instead embrace

a sense of being
tall and with
sharp scent of pine.

In this act there is
always, now,
being and being.

Extremely brief descriptions for esoteric terms:

Dharma right way of living, one's life purpose.

Karma cause and effect; the sum of a person's actions carried into or created in this lifetime.

Koshas the five sheaths, layers of awareness, that begin with the physical body and move towards innermost self.

Lakshmi Hindu goddess of prosperity.

Mantra repeated word, phrase, or sound to aid in meditation.

Rajas one of the three Gunas, qualities of existence inherent in everything. Rajas represents activity/passion.

Tamas one of the three Gunas. Tamas represents inertia/ignorance.

Sattva one of the three Gunas. Sattva represents purity/harmony.

ABOUT THE AUTHOR

Audrey Tanner, Ed.D., is a poet and healer dedicated to the art of self-restoration. As a Reiki Master in the Usui lineage and a certified teacher of yoga and meditation, her writing is an extension of her spiritual practice—a bridge between the physical landscape and the inner soul.

With a doctorate in higher education leadership and over 30 years of university experience, Audrey blends a grounded, scholarly perspective with a deep mastery of Sanskrit mantra and mindfulness. A graduate of the UCLA Extension fiction writing program, she now explores the "quiet magic" of the world through poetry and creative nonfiction. *River Dream* in her invitation to readers to pause, to breathe, and to find oneself reflected in the natural world.

audreytannerwrites.com

MORE BY AUDREY TANNER

SOFT ARRIVALS: Poems from Madeira Island that emerge through Maderia's natural beauty and historic culture. An invitation to the reader to slow down, breathe, and find their way home to themselves.

SLOW MOVING CLOUDS: Poems from Madeira Island that invite the reader into a peaceful experience of awarenesses, imagination, and self-renewal within an atmospheric quietness born of the island's natural beauty.

KARMAS, LIKE HEARTS: A poetry chapbook. Poems about an experience of loss, grief, and recovery that guide the reader with grace from loss to light.

YOU ARE ALWAYS CIRCLING: Meditative poems exploring how the same daily walk reveals connections between nature and self, allowing for peace, self-forgiveness, and revealing what is hidden in the quest to return to innermost self and heart-centered being.